Original title:
Watering the Wild Within

Copyright © 2025 Creative Arts Management OÜ
All rights reserved.

Author: Alexander Thornton
ISBN HARDBACK: 978-1-80581-938-7
ISBN PAPERBACK: 978-1-80581-465-8
ISBN EBOOK: 978-1-80581-938-7

Harmony Amidst the Thorns

In the garden where laughter grows,
A cactus wears a party hose.
The roses dance in socks so bright,
While thorns steal snacks in the moonlight.

Buzzing bees sing silly tunes,
While petals wear their best balloons.
An ant slips on a ladybug,
And both break into a goofy shrug.

Beneath the Canopy of Strangers

Under trees with giggles loud,
A squirrel juggles acorns proud.
With branches tangled like old hair,
Who knew that trees could truly share?

Beneath the shade, a worm does waltz,
While leaves critique his dance with false results.
A stork debates the flight of birds,
As branches snicker ridiculous words.

Threads of Green in the Fabric of Life

A tapestry of leafy waves,
Comedic vines play peek-a-boo braves.
Green threads weave tales of silly strife,
As mushrooms ponder the meaning of life.

The daisies gossip, oh so bold,
About the mix-up with the marigold.
While grasses twist in dance routines,
And share old prickly jokes from queens.

Awakening the Flora of the Heart

In the meadow, hearts take flight,
A daffodil shimmies in delight.
With butterflies sporting goofy hats,
They chuckle at the chatty brats.

A sunflower poses for the sun,
While blowing kisses just for fun.
Together they spin, dance, and clap,
With petals swirling in a mishap.

The Haven of Barefoot Wanderings

In fields where laughter does abound,
I dance through weeds that tickle the ground.
A tiny sprout jives with the breeze,
While butterflies tease with their flitting ease.

A dandelion's wish, I make a shout,
In hopes my dreams will leap about.
But just as I think I'm quite profound,
I trip on a root, what a fall I found!

Chasing my shadow, I stumble and roll,
The earth's soft embrace is a playful console.
I swear I heard chuckles from sun's warm ray,
As I tumble and giggle the afternoon away.

With each silly skip, I shake off my frown,
A merriment feast on this grassy crown.
Among flowers who wink, I declare with cheer,
This haven's laughter, forever near.

Under Currents of Untold Truths

In a puddle deep, my reflection declared,
With a wink and a wave, I was thoroughly scared.
The fish all laughed at my splashy display,
While I tried to make sense of my soggy ballet.

The frogs held a concert, ribbits in the air,
As I danced with two left feet, without a care.
A turtle rolled by, oh so slow,
He grinned at my antics—had quite the show!

With a wiggle and jiggle, I splashed all around,
The water seemed giggly, and so I was bound.
To make a new friend in this liquid embrace,
But I slipped on a leaf, lost my elegant grace!

As bubbles rose high, and the laughter took flight,
I found my adventure in silly delight.
From the depths of the pond, joy leapt anew,
In the currents of chaos, my spirit just grew.

Breathing Life into Silent Echoes

A cactus tried to sing a tune,
With only echoing in a dusty room.
It twirled and danced, oh what a sight,
But the silence laughed, it's not so bright.

The trees were jealous, tried their own jive,
With every sway, they barely survived.
A cast of characters in this oddball show,
Studying how to make silence glow.

Flames of Passion Beneath the Surface

A fish once swam with dreams so grand,
He practiced ballet on golden sand.
But the waves laughed hard, rolling in glee,
'You dance like a fool, it's not meant to be!'

A crab joined in, with rhythm and flair,
Snapping his claws, dancing everywhere.
The reef threw a party, bubbles and cheer,
Who knew the sea held such talent near?

The Essence of Untamed Currents

The river ran wild, with a giggle and cheer,
It splashed the stones, made quite a smear.
"Watch me, watch me!" it bubbled with pride,
"But avoid that tree, it's got quite a ride!"

A turtle grinned, said, "I'll join your spree!"
With a slow-motion shuffle, as smooth as could be.
Together they laughed, the water would sway,
With the essence of jest, brightening the day.

Threads of Hope in the Wilderness

A squirrel with dreams of knitting a nest,
Found yarn in the woods, thought it was the best.
With tangled threads, he reached for the stars,
But all he created were knots and bizarre.

A deer popped in, with grace and poise,
Said, "Why not create with some laughter, not noise?"
So they crafted a cap, a hat made of twigs,
Squirrel wore it proudly, a crown of small digs.

The Secret Alchemy of Growth

In the garden of dreams, I plant my socks,
Hoping they'll bloom into dancing clocks.
Sunshine giggles, rain does a jig,
While worms breakdance, feeling quite big.

A sprout in my fridge, oh what a sight,
Growing between condiments, ready to bite.
I water my fears with lemonade cheer,
And watch them float away on a cold beer.

The Wildness We Long to Know

Chasing butterflies with a cowboy hat,
A flip-flopped hero, a dancing cat.
Running through fields, we embrace the breeze,
Singing with sheep, doing what we please.

A wild umbrella in a soft spring breeze,
It twirls like a dancer atop some trees.
Jumping in puddles, we wear big grins,
In this circus of nature, laughter begins.

Nurturing the Untamed Spirit

Got a pet rock named Rocky, he rolls with glee,
He tells the best jokes, so funny and free.
I feed him my dreams, he nods with delight,
As we plot our adventures from morning till night.

He sprouted a thought, it wobbled and shook,
A wild idea, written in a book.
With crayons we paint our hopes sky-high,
In this madness of joy, we'll never say goodbye.

Secrets of the Whispering Stream

A stream full of giggles runs down the hill,
Telling tall tales that give me a thrill.
With ducks in tuxedos, they waddle and cheer,
As my thoughts take flight, they whisper, "My dear!"

The fish wear sunglasses, quite the slick crew,
They belly flop jokes that'll tickle you too.
In this splashy world, we snicker and play,
Finding joy in the silliest way, every day.

Echoes of a Forgotten Cove

In a cove where seagulls laugh,
Old crabs dance in a conga path.
The waves whisper jokes in the sand,
While fish play pranks that aren't so bland.

A clam burps bubbles, a curious show,
Stars watching with a soft, playful glow.
Jellyfish bounce on a trampoline spree,
As seaweed sways in raucous glee!

Fertile Ground of the Mind

In gardens where daydreams grow tall,
Thoughts bounce like balls in a playful sprawl.
Rusty ideas sprout, oh what a sight,
Like daisies dressed up in disco light!

The weeds crack jokes, if you lean in close,
While daisies gossip like a silly host.
Potatoes eye me with a wink and grin,
"Plant us right, and we'll let the fun begin!"

A Symphony of Nature's Pulse

The trees hum tunes, they can't keep still,
Squirrels add beats with unmatched skill.
A frog croaks a solo, the best in town,
While crickets chirp, never wearing a frown.

The brook tinkles laughter, a cheerful sound,
With flowers clapping, roots dancing around.
In this orchestra, life takes a bow,
Even the clouds join in, singing 'wow!'

Cultivating Dreams in Dappled Light

In shadows where giggles of sunbeams play,
The daisies plot funny things to say.
A butterfly slips in a dress of gold,
While rabbits read jokes from the stories old.

Mushrooms hold parties under old oak trees,
With beetles keeping rhythm, such a tease!
As laughter springs forth like bubbling streams,
Who knew that nature had such wild dreams?

Cry of the Untamed Waves

Splash, splash, the puddles dance,
Frogs in tuxedos take a chance.
They'd leap and croak with all their might,
Wearing boots that fit just right.

Seagulls squawk, they stole my fries,
Diving down from azure skies.
With salty snacks, they try to steal,
Claiming lunch with a beak of steel.

Surfboards wobble, here comes a dude,
Trying to catch waves while munching food.
He flips and falls into the foam,
The ocean shouts, 'Hey, welcome home!'

So grab your bucket, let's make a mess,
Sandy kingdoms we must confess.
Let's wiggle toes and sing a tune,
While seaweed's waltzing to the moon.

Drifting on the Currents of Self

A rubber duck floats, looking grand,
Waving to fish with a tiny hand.
In a whirlpool of thoughts afloat,
He quacks a tune, a bubbly boat.

I'm the captain of this surprise,
Navigating through my own skies.
With cupcakes as my trusty crew,
We sail on waves of chocolate goo.

Socks on my hands, I'm quite the sight,
Paddling hard in a bathtub fight.
With soap suds high, we dance and sway,
Who knew chaos could be this way?

As bubbles burst and laughter rains,
Serenading ducks with silly strains.
Floating dreams on a cotton sea,
Just me, my duck, and inner glee.

Notes from the Edge of Existence

A goldfish wrote a memoir bold,
Of underwater tales retold.
With tiny fins, he took a dive,
Scribbling notes to stay alive.

The cat sat by, all sly and sleek,
Plotting schemes, it's food they seek.
With hopeful eyes, they planned their play,
A bowl of fish awaits today.

In cosmic puddles, stars collide,
Jumping cannonballs from either side.
Fishy laughter fills the air,
As galaxies swirl without a care.

Thus, let us paddle to the brink,
Where chaos spins and we can think.
With quirky tales from far and near,
We'll giggle softly, never fear.

An Infusion of Wilderness Wisdom

An owl wearing glasses just to see,
Hoots out prompts for you and me.
With nature's quirks, his words profound,
He teaches us to look around.

Squirrels debate on what to stash,
And in this chaos, a sudden crash.
Nuts fly high, it's a furry brawl,
As acorns rain down on us all.

The wise old tree starts to sway,
Reciting jokes in a playful way.
Leaves in giggles, branches bend,
The forest whispers, 'Life's a trend!'

With creatures chuckling in the night,
They gather 'round to share delight.
The wild is silly, full of truth,
A laughter infused with nature's youth.

In the Shadow of Ancient Oaks

Beneath the giant trees we lay,
Plotting schemes for play each day.
Squirrels giggle, acorns fall,
Nature's whispers, a raucous call.

We climb with grace, but do we trip?
Branches swing, our laughter's zip.
With every twist, we paint the air,
A circus act, without a care.

The mossy throne feels just like home,
Parrots squawk with tales to roam.
Leaves applaud our little show,
As if they know how wild we glow.

So here we laugh, beneath the light,
In the shade, we're quite the sight.
With ancient oaks as our backdrop,
Life's a jest; we can't quite stop.

Essence of the Untamed

In the fields where daisies dance,
We frolic 'round in silly prance.
With honeybees as our sweet band,
Catching wild dreams, not quite planned.

But when the wind calls out to play,
We tumble forth, come what may.
Butterflies mock with graceful flights,
As we flail like clumsy kites.

The sunbeam tickles our silly toes,
And laughter bursts like wildflowers grows.
With every step, we spark delight,
Unleashing joy that feels so right.

So here's to chaos, to fun, to cheer,
The wild spirit's laughter draws near.
With every folly, we take a stand,
Embracing the essence, bold and grand.

The Language of Wildflowers

Underneath the sky so blue,
Petals gossip while we view.
Dandelions puff and tease,
Spilling secrets in the breeze.

With each bloom, a tale unfolds,
Of buzzing bees and fairy golds.
Sunflowers wink, a cheeky bunch,
While violets giggle in their hunch.

We join the chat, in plant disguise,
Speaking fluent 'flower' surprise.
With dandelion crowns upon our heads,
Embracing whimsy where laughter spreads.

So let us frolic, dance, and sway,
In this wild bouquet, we'll never stray.
For nature's language brings us cheer,
Connecting hearts, both near and dear.

Deep Roots of Resilience

In the soil, where laughter grows,
Dance with roots, strike silly poses.
Through mud and muck, we crawl and slide,
Digging deep with wild pride.

When storms come and branches sway,
We stand tall, come what may.
With a hoot and a holler, we face our fears,
Making mud pies, swapping cheers.

Resilient hearts, in nature's fold,
We find our strength, both brave and bold.
Through every tumble, every fall,
We rise again, we heed the call.

So here we thrive, with joyous tease,
In every whisper of the breeze.
With roots deep-set, in laughter's tone,
We bloom our wildness, ours alone.

Nurturing the Untamed Spirit

In the garden where the weeds play,
I try to chat, make them stay.
They giggle as I offer tea,
But all they want is more of me.

The daisies dance, so full of cheer,
Claiming the sunlight near and dear.
While daisies gossip, I just grin,
At their wild tales of where they've been.

A rogue tomato, red and round,
Insists it's king of underground.
I bow to his regal haughty strut,
While squirrels cheer, 'You're such a nut!'

An orange carrot tries to waltz,
But trips on dirt and slowly halts.
I laugh and cheer, 'Next time you'll shine!'
It bows with pride, "I still feel fine!"

Subterranean Streams of Growth

Down below, the earthworms spin,
Debating who will win this win.
They rattle tales of roots and grubs,
While ants parade with tiny tubs.

Mice hold court with acorns tall,
Arguing which is best of all.
Each nut the size of their small heads,
You'd think they're hoarding beds instead!

A toad sits back, arms crossed in style,
Watching others raccoon and rile.
He croaks, 'You kids need time to chill,'
But still he jumps, just for the thrill.

Beneath the surface, laughter flows,
As seeds prepare for their great shows.
They wink and nod with leafy might,
While wishing on a starry night.

Blossoms Beneath the Moonlight

The moon spills silver on the grass,
Where flowers fuss and feign to class.
'Look at me, I'm posh and bright!'
But all I see is pure delight.

A daisy swears she's royalty,
While dandelions laugh with glee.
'You call yourself a flower, dear?'
While winking, they spread joy and cheer.

An owl hoots jokes from up on high,
Sneaking swigs from a pie in the sky.
'I'm wisdom!' he claims with such class,
While shoveling bites right from the glass.

The night whispers with playful blooms,
As jokes blossom in moonlit rooms.
Each petal tickles the air with glee,
In this garden, wild and free.

Reawakening the Forest Soul

The trees all gather for a chat,
Discussing who is tall or flat.
Birch likes to boast of her sleek style,
While pines just chuckle, 'It's just a mile!'

A squirrel struts as self-proclaimed king,
While blossoms giggle at everything.
He stashes nuts, his royal bling,
But mostly dreams of springtime fling.

Mushrooms cluster, trying to shine,
Claiming the secrets of the divine.
'We're the tastiest, just you wait!'
But everyone laughs, 'You're just bait!'

Ferns wave gently, a stylish show,
Bowing softly, putting on a glow.
In this wood, where laughter flows,
The wild awakens with quirky shows.

The Garden of Inside Out

In a garden where my thoughts collide,
Blooming jokes and puns reside.
Weeds of worry, I shall uproot,
With laughter's shovel, oh what a hoot!

The daisies chuckle, the roses grin,
While under the sun, I spin and spin.
Even cacti tease with prickly wit,
In this patch, there's no need to sit!

Bumblebees buzz with a comic flair,
While butterflies dance without a care.
The sun beams down, a spotlight bright,
On this show, I'm the star tonight!

So let's plant joy in every row,
A garden where silly seeds can grow.
With every giggle, our roots entwine,
In the garden of the silly and divine!

Whispered Secrets in the Wind

The breeze brings secrets, or so they say,
Flavored jokes from afar, on display.
I catch them like butterflies, soft and light,
Twisting through trees, it's quite a sight!

The wind's a joker, it flits and flies,
Tickling leaves and making them sighs.
It whispers pranks from each swaying vine,
Twirling around, it's always on time!

Clouds join in, wearing smiles so bloated,
With raindrops laughing, the sky corroded.
A river chuckles, don't let it be shy,
As it tumbles downstream, waving goodbye!

In this forest of whispers and giggles galore,
Each gust of wind knows the best folklore.
So let's dance with the breezes and twirl in the air,
For in nature's humor, we all share!

Tending to the Inner Wilderness

I stumble through jungles of my own mind,
Untamed thoughts and dreams intertwined.
With a rake of humor and a spade of glee,
I dig for the treasure that's waiting for me!

Vines of laughter grow wild and free,
While shrubs of silliness beckon with glee.
I prune my worries with a joke or two,
In this wild place, there's always a brew!

But beware of the monkeys that swing through the trees,
They steal my snacks and laugh with the breeze.
Yet their antics make me chuckle and grin,
In this wilderness, we all fit in!

So let's plant our quirks and dance with delight,
In this expansive nature, everything's right.
With each funny twist, this journey we share,
Exploring the wild that bubbles out there!

The Burgeoning Heartbeat of Nature

Nature thumps with a giggly beat,
Where flowers bloom and dance on their feet.
The trees sway gently, a cheerful song,
A concert of chuckles where all belong!

The roots tap dance in the earthy ground,
As laughter rises, sweet and profound.
A playful breeze plays the flute,
Inviting me to join the route!

Squirrels prance with flair and grace,
While frogs croak out in a rhyming race.
Bubbles of joy rise from lakes so bright,
In this ecosystem, every joke takes flight!

So tune in closely, feel that thrum,
The heartbeat of nature, all bouncing in fun.
With each chuckle, we're part of the spree,
In this lively rhythm, just you and me!

Streams That Sing of Strife

In a brook where thoughts collide,
The fish hold meetings, side by side.
They gossip 'bout the bait that's lost,
And plot to teach the worms who's boss.

With splashes that break the tense debates,
The currents twist and weave their fates.
A dragonfly rolls its eyes and sighs,
While water spiders share the latest lies.

Across the rocks, they dance with flair,
A sight so odd, it draws a stare.
Each ripple hums a tune so bold,
Of flippers, fins, and tales retold.

So if you catch a thought gone wild,
Just blame the stream; it's nature's child.
They swim and splash, in gleeful fight,
A symphony of chaos, pure delight.

The Fertile Ground of Reflection

In puddles deep, where thoughts can stew,
The frogs hold meetings—who knew?
They ponder life, they joke, they croak,
As dragonflies join in their smoke.

A worm wiggles, wanting in,
The frogs yell out, "Don't be so thin!"
As laughter echoes through the mud,
"Let's make a plan to tie a flood!"

Reflections show their quirky sides,
As shadows dance on lily tides.
A fish sneezes, sending waves,
Of giggles in the muck, how brave!

In this fine muck, ideas bloom,
As frogs and friends make merry room.
The wisdom here is clear and bright,
Laugh loud and let your heart take flight!

An Oasis in the Wilderness

In a desert dry, a cactus sneezes,
While lizards laugh, and time just freezes.
They say, "Let's start a water fight!"
But none can find a drop tonight.

A mirage flickers—oh, what a tease!
The camels join in, trying to squeeze.
They splash through sand, as if in jest,
Dancing around, they think they're blessed.

Then from afar, a traveler calls,
As tumbleweeds weave, and laughter sprawls.
"I found the fountain!" they shout with glee,
But it's just a puddle—a sight to see!

So in this place where parched dreams play,
A chuckle dances in the sun's bright ray.
For in the wild, where mirth is rare,
The joy of thirst can spark a flare.

Echoes of the Untamed Spirit

In the woods where tall trees lean,
Squirrels argue, trying to glean.
They chirp and chatter, tails on end,
Their acorns stacked like reasons to mend.

An owl hoots, "You've missed the mark!"
While raccoons play like a band in the dark.
They tiptoe through leaves, a clumsy quest,
While critters conspire, never a rest.

The whispers carry through dense foliage,
As nature laughs in playful homage.
A twig snaps loud; all heads turn quick,
It's just the wind playing a trick!

With echoes bouncing, the spirit is free,
Chasing the laughter of every tree.
So if you wander, join in the cheer—
Raise your voice loud—let the wild steer!

The Wildness Beneath Our Feet

In the soil, secrets hide,
With worms beneath, full of pride.
Rabbits hop, a game of chase,
They giggle in their furry race.

Sneaky beetles on a spree,
Teasing flowers, "Look at me!"
Roots are dancing, shaking hands,
While sprouts discuss their travel plans.

Twirling leaves join in the fun,
Playing tag till the day is done.
Nature's party, wild and free,
Join the giggles, come and see!

Underfoot, life skips and plays,
In muddy puddles, we will stay.
With all these friends, who needs a map?
Let's embrace this nature lap!

Petals of Passion in the Breeze

Daisies whisper sweetly loud,
Petals bask, they feel so proud.
Butterflies wear cheerful grins,
As they showcase their colorful skins.

Tulips sway with giddy glee,
In the wind, just like a spree.
Buzzing bees join in the dance,
While flowers share a breezy chance.

Rosehips giggle, 'Look at me!'
Seductive colors, can't you see?
A daffodil tries to tell a joke,
But it falls flat, oh funny bloke!

In this garden, humor blooms,
With nature's quirks, we shake the rooms.
Petals flutter, laughter's call,
In this place, there's fun for all!

Sowing Seeds of Inner Exploration

Plant a dream in a tiny pot,
Water it—just don't spill a lot!
Watch it sprout with all its might,
A quirky dance, a humorous sight.

Digging deep, I find some gold,
Or maybe just a sock, I'm told.
In the dirt, lost treasures lurk,
With each shovel, let's go berserk!

Seeds of laughter, seeds of cheer,
Planted deeply, never fear.
Each sprout a giggle, each root a pun,
Finding joy in the springtime sun.

Grow your whims; let them fly,
Watch them twirl and reach the sky.
In this field of funny seeds,
Who needs a map when humor leads?

Currents of Freedom Rising

Waves of giggles crash on shores,
As seagulls dive, the freedom soars.
Sandy toes and sun-kissed skin,
In this world, we simply grin.

Splashing puddles, laughter loud,
Who would trade this fun for a crowd?
The ocean calls, let's take a ride,
On floating dreams, let's slip and slide.

Tides of joy with every wave,
Seashells singing, trying to save.
In salty breezes, we lose our cares,
Playing hide and seek with friendly airs.

In the deep, the freedom flows,
As dolphins dance and chaos grows.
Ride the current, feel the tease,
As we laugh in the ocean breeze!

Beneath the Arching Skies

Cacti dance under the earnest sun,
Wearing hats that are quite overdone.
Their prickly arms waving in glee,
As the clouds play hide-and-seek with the sea.

Birds gossip loudly about neighborly theft,
A worm stole their snack, oh what a heft!
They squawk and they flutter, a comical site,
While the sun sets, bathing the day in light.

Even the daisies sprout silly chins,
While rabbits hop round with mischievous grins.
Each blade of grass tickles toes on the go,
In a goofy parade, all putting on a show.

Beneath the arching skies, the laughter will flow,
As nature conspires to steal the whole show.
With every odd blossom that raises a cheer,
The world spins on joy, from far and from near.

Chronicles of the Earthbound Heart

A snail wrote a letter, it took all night,
To tell of his journey, what a brave sight!
He climbed a tall hill, then tripped on a stone,
After all that, he found he liked home.

The ants threw a party without any cake,
With crumbs from above, they danced for a break.
Their tiny parade was a sight quite absurd,
As they marched to the beat of one overly loud bird.

Bees buzzing gossip about flowers so fine,
Sipped nectar cocktails like they were divine.
One bee got tipsy and danced on a petal,
Creating quite a ruckus—a hummingbird medal!

In tales of the earthbound, we find our own cheer,
Adventure awaits, not far, but quite near.
Each laugh that escapes from critters so light,
Brings echoes of joy to the whispering night.

The Worn Path of the Brave

On a path lined with twigs, a squirrel juggles nuts,
With a grin on his face, he eludes any cuts.
He stumbles, he fumbles, the audience roars,
As acorns go flying, it's chaos outdoors!

A raccoon peeks in, with a mask so refined,
Looking for snacks, he's rather aligned.
He finds leftover pizza, a treasure so rare,
With a flick of his paw, he insists on a share.

The wind brings a tickle, it laughs through the trees,
While a frog in a pond croaks about ease.
He floats on a lily, declaring it's grand,
To be king of the pond, with no need for a band.

Along the worn path, they jest and they play,
Each critter a hero, brightening the day.
For in every mishap, a giggle will bloom,
Crafting tales of the wild, dispelling the gloom.

Glimmers of Light in the Underbrush

The fireflies flicker with sheer jubilation,
Hosting a dance, a bright celebration.
They twirl in the night, like stars caught in flight,
Leading the critters to join the delight.

A hedgehog rolled by, in pursuit of a dream,
He tripped on a root, letting out a loud scream.
The laughter cascaded through leaves and wide logs,
As the dance floor filled with an army of frogs!

In shadows they whispered, wild stories anew,
Of journeys they took, and the bait that they flew.
The tale of the turtle who thought he could race,
(But fell asleep first; what a shameful disgrace!)

Amid glimmers of light, friendships take flight,
With every new giggle, the world feels more bright.
In the underbrush laughter fills every nook,
As twilight spins magic in this joyous book.

The Thirst for Authentic Connection

In a world of filtered smiles,
We chase the truth like lost cats.
A handshake's better than likes,
But leave the selfies for the brats.

When connections twist like pretzels,
We search for tangents, not the bends.
A nod, a joke, a riddle speaks,
True friends will always need amends.

With mismatched socks and silly hats,
We gather round for goofy chats.
The joy of clumsiness is clear,
Authenticity brings the cheer!

A sip of tea, a dance in rain,
We let the quirks drive us insane.
In laughter's spark, we find desire,
Connection's flame—our friendship fire!

Unfurling the Veil of the Unknown

In shadows deep where mysteries lurk,
We wiggle like worms in the dirt.
Peeking behind the veil so sly,
Who knew chaos could giggle and squirt?

With slippery paths and chocolate pies,
The unknown tickles our curious eyes.
We step with caution, hearts a'flutter,
Every jump is a chance to mutter!

Banana peels and cosmic jokes,
Dancing through dreams like silly folk.
Inquirers at heart, we take the leap,
Unfurling secrets that make us weep.

A treasure quest in pajamas bold,
We navigate wonders yet untold.
With mischief woven into our plight,
The unknown wraps us tight, so right!

From Shadows to Shimmering Shore

From shadows deep, we craved the sand,
Where sun rays tickle and seaweed stands.
Waves crash laughter against our toes,
As we hunt for crabs and pose like pros.

The flip-flop flops, the sunscreen flies,
We dance through puddles, splash from the skies.
In quirky hats and goggles worn,
We embrace the joy of summer's dawn.

From dim to bright, a wobbly path,
We make grand stories, and sometimes math.
And when the tide pulls us back in,
We spin like tops, where giggles begin.

With starfish friends and jelly-fish foes,
We celebrate life in whimsical shows.
From shadows cast, to shores we pour,
Together we giggle, forevermore!

The Cradle of Wilderness Secrets

In a cradle of trees where whispers sleep,
We find the secrets the wildlings keep.
With squirrels gossiping and owls that hoot,
Every adventure comes with a boot!

The mushrooms giggle, the winds do sing,
A showdown of nature—a wild fling.
We crush leaf piles and jump with glee,
Unruly beasts of chaos run free.

Among the ferns and backflipping frogs,
We craft a tale with imaginary dogs.
Cache of treasures in every nook,
The secrets spill from each little crook.

With a snicker and shriek, we brave each night,
In the cradle of wilderness, oh what a sight!
With fairies' laughter and moonbeams bright,
We frame the chaos; life feels so right!

Streams of Consciousness Unfolding

A river of thoughts flows quite absurd,
Like fish in a hurry, each word is stirred.
Bubbles of laughter dance on the way,
As my brain takes a stroll, come join in the play.

The currents tickle my toes in delight,
Like ducks wearing shoes in a quirky sight.
Splashing around with a giggle or two,
Who knew my own mind could make such a hue?

Ideas like rafts float by, oh so bold,
Some made of candy, some made of gold.
I catch them with nets fashioned from dreams,
Laughing at nonsense, or so it seems.

So grab a life vest and join me today,
In this stream of fun, where thoughts dance and sway.
We'll paddle through whimsy, and feel quite alive,
Chasing the currents where giggles can thrive.

The Untrodden Path of Self-Discovery

I wander a path that twists and bends,
Where squirrels debate and a cactus pretends.
The rocks make me giggle with every strange hop,
Is it wisdom I seek, or just a fun stop?

A sign says 'this way' but points to the sky,
While birds hold a meeting, oh me, oh my!
I trip over flowers that whisper in code,
Maybe 'finding myself' needs a lighter load.

With a backpack of snacks and a hat full of dreams,
I march on the trail with laughter in beams.
In this jungle of thoughts, my compass is lost,
But finding a funny hat is well worth the cost.

So let's frolic together, unearth all the fun,
In this quirky adventure, we'll never outrun.
Each twist is a giggle, each turn is a jest,
On this untrodden path, we're truly the best.

When Roots Embrace the Sky

The trees throw their arms up, waving hello,
While roots play tag with the grass down below.
Clouds tickle branches, quite silly, I'm told,
As laughter escapes from the saplings so bold.

Roots forming friendships, they wiggle with glee,
"Let's touch those big clouds, they're so fluffy!"
A dance of the ages, a merry sway,
While squirrels zoom past like they're in a ballet.

Sunshine spills down like a joyful parade,
While leaves crack a joke under the shade.
"Who knew being grounded could feel so free?
Let's grow a bit taller, come climb with me!"

And as night falls gently with stars up so high,
The roots whisper secrets that float through the sky.
In a world full of laughter, where trees play and sigh,
It's a hoot when the roots decide to fly!

Petals of the Unseen Realm

In a garden of giggles where petals roll deep,
Blooming in laughter, not a secret to keep.
Each flower a joke that's just waiting to burst,
Tickling the air with its whimsy and thirst.

The daisies are trading their best punchlines,
While tulips join in, sipping on good times.
A rose stops to chat, says, "I'm no mere thorn,
I'm a crown made for laughter, from dusk until morn!"

In this unseen realm where petals all laugh,
Butterflies wobble like they're on a path.
"Here comes the sun!" shouts the daffodil crew,
Lighting up smiles like the dawn's golden hue.

So wander with me through this floral delight,
Where petals of humor bring joy to the night.
In gardens of laughter, where fun's always near,
We'll bloom ever brighter, shedding all fear.

Chasing Ripples of Restlessness

In a pond of patience I take a leap,
The fish start laughing, oh what a peep!
They bubble and chuckle, swim with glee,
I'm just a splashy fool, can't let it be.

Tadpoles flip their tiny tails in cheer,
As I chase my thoughts that disappear.
The water's like a stage, I'm the clown,
Flopping around in my oversized gown.

The frogs join the chorus, croak a refrain,
My antics create a delightful campaign.
With each little ripple, humor expands,
Nature's own jesters, with wiggly bands.

So here's to the madness, both wet and wild,
In the dance of the silly, I remain a child.
With every splash, a chuckle resounds,
In this watery playground, absurdity abounds.

In the Shade of Untamed Canopies

Under leafy umbrellas, squirrels play tag,
Chasing their tails, they wag and brag.
I sip from a coconut, feeling quite wise,
While the birds gossip beneath sunny skies.

A raccoon critiques my not-so-smooth dance,
I'll show him moves he won't dare to chance!
The branches sway as if to conspire,
To turn my missteps into a lively choir.

The sun throws a party, invites every bug,
I'm swatting at shadows, feeling quite snug.
As laughter erupts in a rustling hum,
I trip on a root, and then start to run.

In the shade, we're all misfits, quite free,
The wild ones here, so lively and spree.
I tip my coconut, what a delightful scene,
With nature's laughter, it's the best routine.

A Symphony of Nature's Yearning

The trees are musicians with branches as bows,
Playing a symphony where the wild wind blows.
I'm a mere audience, caught in the fun,
As the leaves whisper secrets under the sun.

The crickets join in with a chirping spree,
Adding their notes, oh so cheekily.
From behind a rock, a lizard takes lead,
Strumming like a boss, nature's true breed.

Each rustle and roll is a comedic play,
As the blues of the sky start taking their sway.
I giggle at raindrops as they start to dance,
In this symphonic world, I'll take my chance.

With every chord struck, I wiggle and sway,
In the concert of nature, I'm here to stay.
So let the wild play its funny, silly tune,
Where humor and wildness create the monsoon.

The Pulse of Existential Currents

Floating on thoughts like a leaf on a stream,
Caught in the current, I ponder and dream.
The fish roll their eyes at my ponderous ways,
While bubbles tease me with their cheeky displays.

A turtle swims by, gives a knowing grin,
I ask him for wisdom, he just reels in.
He's seen life's questions, but shrugs with a laugh,
"Just ride with the flow, it's a watery path!"

The river whispers secrets in rippling tones,
I'm lost in its laughter, imagining homes.
Snakes do the cha-cha and owls throw their hoots,
As I fumble through life in my polka dot boots.

So here's to the currents, both wild and absurd,
My existential musings fly like a bird.
With the pulse of nature, I'm bound to break free,
In this jolly adventure, just let it all be.

Uncharted Waters of Emotion

In puddles I splash, oh what a delight,
Making waves in my mind, things feel so light.
With a rubber duck ship, I set sail today,
Charting courses through laughter, come join my play!

Giggling at currents that twist and bend,
Each giggle a boat, every chortle a friend.
Throw me a life vest, but only if it's bright,
For the seas of my heart are a comical sight!

Bubbles rise high, like my hopes and dreams,
Floating away on whimsical streams.
Catch me a wave or just let it flow,
As we ride on the tides of a chuckling show!

So aboard this ship, let your worries disperse,
We'll navigate laughter, for better or worse.
In uncharted waters, we'll dance with glee,
A splash of the funny is all that we need!

Reclaiming the Forgotten Garden

In the backyard jungle, weeds dance a jig,
With gnomes as my witnesses, I'll dig and dig.
Beneath all the chaos, seeds yearn for a chance,
To blossom in beauty, perhaps with a prance!

A sunflower whispered, 'Let's plot a coup!'
Someone left the gate open; let's break through!
With each poke and prod, we're holding a feast,
A garden of giggles, to say the least!

While tomatoes complain, 'Too much sun, oh dear!'
The carrots are plotting, 'Let's disappear!'
But a juicy convo makes all things bright,
As we argue and banter through day and night.

So pull up a weed, and let's have a laugh,
We'll reclaim this green space, half row, half path.
With worms as our buddies, it's quite the formation,
In this forgotten garden, we make jubilation!

The Elixir of Hidden Desires

In a potion shop, I found a strange brew,
"Drink for your secrets!" said a wizard, how new.
With a swirl and a twirl, the odd colors blend,
It tickles my taste buds, what's about to send?

A sip fills my heart with each bubbling cheer,
Laughter erupts, oh, what's hiding in here?
Confessions of cookies and dance-off regrets,
Whispers of dreams that I cannot forget.

I tasted my wishes, they tasted like pie,
And a sprinkle of mischief that flew right on by.
With each burp and giggle, I'm feeling alive,
The elixirs of folly help my hopes thrive!

So let's brew a laugh with a side of delight,
As we sip on the wonders that dance in the night.
In this magical coffer, our impulses conspire,
To turn all my giggles into glorious fire!

Transcendence Through Simple Touch

A pat on the back, oh what a sensation,
Sparks of delight, a joyful vibration.
With fingers like wands, we conjure a smile,
In the land of the silly, let's stay for a while!

A high-five explosion, what fun it can create,
Like fireworks of laughter, they never wait.
Squeezes and tickles, the simple and sweet,
Each touch makes us giggle, life's little treat!

Walking a tightrope of playful finesse,
Avoiding the footsie of impending distress.
Embraces that tumble, laughter like snow,
As we frolic in moments, let our joy flow.

Together we leap, like kangaroos in charge,
In the world of affection, our spirits enlarge.
Through simple connections, our hearts can ignite,
Transcend into laughter, oh what a delight!

The Quench of Life's Paradox

A cactus asked for lemonade,
But all it got was shade.
The river laughed, it liked to tease,
Refreshing pool, a desert ease.

A fish once dreamed of flying high,
With fins adorned and feathered tie.
It put on wings, dived with a splash,
Only to end in a fishy crash.

An octopus tried to dance a jig,
With eight left feet, and quite the big.
It twirled and swirled, what a sight,
But inked itself in sheer delight.

A frog made soup from pond's delight,
And dined alone beneath the bright.
But every spoonful made him croak,
Not every dish is built for joke.

Beyond the Verge of the Known

A snail set sail, quite the bold trip,
Thought of a cruise, not a slip.
But halfway there, found no crew,
Just a leaf, a wayward view.

A squirrel took up physics class,
To learn the secrets of the grass.
It jumped to learn how to defy,
Ended up stuck in a pie, oh my!

A turtle wore a top hat with flair,
Claiming elegance, unaware.
It slipped on moss, who'd have thought,
Fashion fails in puddles caught.

A bee who dreamt of being a chef,
Buzzed recipes for that very quest.
But made a mess of honeyed dough,
Instead of cakes, it stole the show!

Illuminating Hidden Pathways

A glowworm tried to host a rave,
But ended up a disco wave.
With friends like beetles, who all showed,
They danced till dawn on the darkened road.

A raccoon donned a bandit mask,
To steal some treats and hide from task.
But every snack was wrapped in foil,
He had to juggle—what a toil!

The moonlit path was lined with dreams,
With shadow dancers and starlit beams.
A shadow slipped and missed the groove,
Tripping over, trying to move.

A chameleon changed its skin to fun,
Merging colors, everyone's done.
But in a rush, forgot the hue,
Stuck in stripes, oh what a view!

The Flow of Untold Stories

A riverbank had tales to tell,
Of fishy romances, oh so swell.
But every time it tried to spill,
A frog croaked loudly, 'Let me thrill!'

A waterfall's song was lost in mist,
Yearning for notes of a twist.
But all the rocks just laughed away,
In echoing humor, brightening day.

A raindrop planned a Broadway play,
With puddles cast in chanson sway.
But slipped on stage, went off-script,
And turned the show into a blip!

An ocean wave craved poetry,
But every line was a mystery.
It wrote a verse, then crashed ashore,
Splattering ideas, wanting more!

Labyrinths of the Heart's Desire

In the maze of love I roam,
Chasing echoes that feel like home.
With chocolate crumbs, my path is set,
A sweet diversion, my heart's duet.

Round and round, I spin and twirl,
A dizzy dance, a heartfelt whirl.
Lost in thoughts, where giggles flow,
What's next in this romantic show?

Each corner turns, a surprise unplanned,
A rubber chicken in my hand.
With silly hats and laughter bright,
I wander 'til I find my light.

So here I stand, my heart aglow,
Lost in love's odd, silly show.
In labyrinths of dreams, I play,
And hope the snacks won't fade away.

Pursuit of the Unseen

I chased a ghost on a whim one day,
Hoping it would join my festive fray.
With pizza slices and tunes so fine,
I promised drinks—just one more wine!

In the shadows, it danced and laughed,
While I tripped over my own daft craft.
A wild pursuit of a phantom bold,
I've caught more slips than tales retold.

Through kitchen drawers and tangled sheets,
I asked the cat for helpful cheats.
With eyes aglow, it simply sighed,
"You're on your own, enjoy the ride!"

Yet deeper still, into the night,
I chased that ghost with sheer delight.
Each step, a giggle, each fall, a cheer,
In the unseen realm, I lose all fear.

The Harmony of Nature's Chords

In the meadow, bugs join in,
With tiny drums that make me grin.
A squirrel solo, on a high branch,
Nature's band in a lively dance.

Flowers sway in vibrant hues,
While bumblebees hum their funky blues.
A frog croaks out a quirky jam,
It's a wild song; oh, did I say 'ham'?

Each rustle's part of a silly score,
As rabbits choreograph, needing more.
With wings aflutter, a bluebird sings,
Nature's concert—oh, how it swings!

So let us dance 'neath a leafy dome,
With wild, funny friends, we call this home.
In harmony, we find our way,
In laughter and song, we choose to stay.

Rebirth Amongst the Blossoms

Out from winter's cold embrace,
I burst forth with a funny face.
In bloom, I forget the frosty chill,
With bright green sprouts and a ticklish thrill.

The daffodils giggle as they poke,
While I trip on roots and giggle, oh, choke!
Butterflies wink with their vibrant flair,
Do they know what's hiding in my hair?

Every petal whispers cheerful tunes,
I dance along beneath the moon.
A garden party, where laughs are free,
Rebirth in blooms—come celebrate with me!

So here's to spring, a wild debut,
With croaky frogs and sky so blue.
We'll laugh and twirl till the sunlight fades,
Amongst the blossoms, joy cascades.

Cultivating Chaos in Calm

In stillness lies a bubbling brew,
A dance of squirrels, a breaker crew.
With shaking leaves, the gossip flows,
While clever crows in jackets pose.

A juggler's flair in muddy shoes,
They flip and twirl, forget the blues.
Planting seeds of mischief wide,
While giggling blooms wear grinning pride.

The sun slips in, a prankster's grin,
Tickling daisies for a swim.
A sprinkler springs, just like a clown,
Splashing puddles, upside down.

Roots like sneakers, tangled spree,
Who knew nature could be so free?
In chaos, harmony finds its place,
As grasshoppers join the merry chase.

The Meadow's Gentle Embrace

Oh, the meadow sways with swirls of cheer,
Where butterflies flirt and grass sings near.
Bumblebees buzzing with grand finesse,
Wearing pollen jackets, no need to impress.

A rabbit hops in a zigzag race,
With a radish stuck in his funny face.
Daffodils giggle, sun shining bright,
As daisies dance, oblivious to fright.

The breeze has jokes, tickles the trees,
Who chuckle and shimmy, swaying with ease.
A game of tag, leaf to leaf,
Nature's comedy, a sweet relief.

As clouds roll in, a fluffy parade,
Raindrops tap-dancing, fun never delayed.
In the meadow's arms, laughter unfurls,
Where all of nature's delight twirls.

Awakening Nature's Heart

A rooster crows with a cartoonish flair,
Waking up flowers too stubborn to care.
Fluffy clouds drift, plotting their play,
As morning light teases where dreams lay.

The pond reflects a pirate's glee,
As frogs take bets in a singing spree.
Tadpoles twirling in elegant arcs,
Create splashy concerts with ribbits and larks.

A mischievous fox in a ballet leap,
Chasing his tail, a secret to keep.
With nature's ticker tape parade,
The wild inside us serenely played.

With sun-tickled leaves, joy fills the air,
As crickets crack jokes without a care.
Here in chaos, we all find our start,
The laughter twinkles, awakening the heart.

Tendrils of the Untouched Soul

In hidden groves where whispers linger,
Trees tell tales with their leafy finger.
While mushrooms giggle in polka dot hats,
And ants march proudly, wearing their stats.

A secret world beneath our feet,
Dancing shadows in a glorious beat.
With roots that twist in a tangled song,
Nature's chorus feels so very strong.

A shy deer peeks with a curious eye,
Sprinkling laughter as she trots by.
With each little sprout, a jest unfurls,
As dandelions share their fluffs and swirls.

In this untouched, wild domain,
Miracles spring with the slightest rain.
Tendrils winding, a joyous role,
Beneath it all, the playful soul.

The Tide of Unexplored Horizons

A rubber duck floats with pride,
In seas of glitter, where dreams collide.
Paddling backwards, what a sight!
Laughing at waves that tickle with might.

Fish wear hats and throw confetti,
Crabs in tuxedos, oh so ready!
Underwater disco, fish dance free,
With jellyfish jiving—oh, let it be!

Seagulls sport shades, sipping on brine,
While octopuses paint; it's simply divine.
A tide of giggles, a splashy spree,
Who knew the ocean held such glee?

A message inside a bottle floats by,
"Send more ice cream!" it pleads; oh my!
In this absurdity, joy runs wide,
In unexplored horizons, let's take a ride!

Gazing into Nature's Soul

Squirrels with spectacles read the news,
While bunnies plot their next big snooze.
In stillness, a whisper of leaves shall say,
Nature's giggles lighten the day.

Frogs in togas hold fashion shows,
Rabbits hop like they own the O's.
Gazing up high, we see the trees,
Trading tales with the buzzing bees.

The breeze cracks jokes as it blows past,
Tickling noses, it moves so fast.
With trees as the audience, all in a row,
Nature's comedy is the best kind of show!

Beneath the clouds, a carnival awaits,
With rainbows and laughter — oh, what great mates!
Nature invites us to join her scroll,
In the comedy club of a wandering soul.

Spark of Life Amidst the Wild

A butterfly flutters on a sock that's lost,
With pollen parties, they dance at all cost.
Bees don bow ties, all spruced up right,
While ants throw confetti in pure delight.

A raccoon with dreams of stardom bright,
Steals the show with a moonlit bite.
Twinkling stars above, they cheer and beam,
As nature's rascals plot their wild dream.

A snappy turtle claims a frazzled hat,
"Why rush through life? Just check out that!"
With laughter echoing through tangled vines,
In perennial parties, joy intertwines.

Each brook trickles tales with a splash and a frown,
Then bursts into giggles as it tumbles down.
In this lively wild, let laughter ignite,
The spark of life shines oh so bright!

Serene Chaos Beneath the Stars

The stars are snickering, what's that they see?
A goat on a skateboard, wild and free!
In a moonlit meadow, a circus unfolds,
Where owls juggle fire and stories are told.

Crickets play banjo, frogs hum along,
While the fireflies glow, casting magic so strong.
A raccoon in pajamas leads dances so grand,
In serene chaos, all lend a hand.

A breeze may trip over its own flow,
Laughing at night as it swirls to and fro.
Under the cosmos, laughter takes flight,
With comets that giggle, oh what a sight!

So join in the fun, beneath the vast sky,
Find the joy hidden where stars like to lie.
In chaotic beauty, we lose track of time,
As nature serenades with laughter and rhyme!

The Wildflower's Renascence

In the meadow where daisies laugh,
A squirrel slips by, on a floral path.
He wears a hat made of leaves and twigs,
Dancing round like he's had too many jigs.

Butterflies flutter, trying to impress,
While ants hold a summit, a conference mess.
"Who stole my crumb?!" yells a little ant,
While a ladybug giggles, saying, "Oh, not a chance!"

The sun peeks in, tickling each bloom,
A wise old toad croaks, "Let's make room!"
For a party of creatures, both shy and bold,
Where stories of gardens and wilds are told.

So raise a glass made of petal and dew,
To the chaos of life, and the antics anew.
For every wildflower, in its own time,
Will dance and will laugh, in prose and in rhyme.

Echoing Lullabies of the Thicket

In the thicket where shadows play,
The fox sings softly, "Hey, hey, hey!"
With a rhythm that jiggles the leaves above,
Even the owls can't help but shove!

A rabbit hops in, with style so grand,
Wearing a cloak made from a soft band.
"Is it a fashion show?" he declares with flair,
While the chipmunk squeaks, "Take it elsewhere, air!"

Beneath the glimmer of the moon's soft glow,
The creatures all gather to put on a show.
"Let's sing, let's dance, let's make it a night,"
As hedgehogs spin under stars shining bright.

With laughter and giggles, the thicket does sway,
As everyone joins in the wild cabaret.
In echoes of joy, all the worries take flight,
In a world that's alive with pure heart and delight.

The Hidden Sanctum of Desire

In the nook of the garden, secrets unfold,
Where snails leave their trails, and the gossip gets bold.
"Did you see that bee? What a vibrant show!"
Said the sunflower cheekily, "Oh, I know, I know!"

Violets gossip while the wind makes a scene,
"Who wears that color? Oh, it's just evergreen!"
Each bloom shares a secret, each petal a tale,
As the breezes swirl round like a playful gale.

In this hidden space where desire runs free,
The rocks hum a tune, a sweet harmony.
A lady's wish floating like bubbles in tea,
"Let's drink to the moments, so wild and so free!"

So cheers to the garden, so vibrant and spry,
With laughter ringing louder than whispers nearby.
For in every petal, a wink and a sway,
Are dreams that awaken, come dance and play!

Nurture in the Dance of Rain

When raindrops begin to laugh on the ground,
A troupe of seedlings spin round and round.
"Is this a shower or an aquatic ballet?"
The carrots chuckle, "Come join us, okay?"

The puddles reflect a dance so absurd,
As worms wiggle by, singing their word.
"Spot the splash dance, your moves are so slick!"
To a beetle who twirls, feeling oh-so-quick!

The clouds tumble down, spilling giggles galore,
Every droplet invites to come dance some more.
With the rhythm of nature, they flounce in delight,
While frogs croak their chorus, what a silly sight!

So let's sway with the rain, feel the joy in the air,
For even the flowers know how to be fair.
With a tap of their petals, they hum and they play,
In the muddy embrace of a wet and wild day!

Unfolding Layers of the Heart

Beneath my chest, a garden grows,
Where every giggle tickles my toes.
Each layer peels like an onion's skin,
Oh, what laughter's trapped within!

With rubber ducks, I navigate dreams,
In puddles of joy, or so it seems.
A heart that blooms like a sunflower,
Can giggle louder than a shower!

Hidden treasures lie in each fold,
A tale of silliness waiting to unfold.
With polka dots and mismatched shoes,
My heart sings songs, it can't refuse!

So grab a shovel, let's dig the art,
Of finding fun in every part.
The layers spin like a whirling bird,
While the world giggles; haven't you heard?

The Lantern of Wayward Streams

A lantern bobbles on the brook,
Guiding lost socks that no one took.
It flickers bright with a silly beam,
Splitting the night with a giggly gleam!

Fish wear hats and dance in line,
To the sound of water, sipping fine wine.
The lanterns laugh as they waddle along,
In this odd parade, they all belong!

Do frogs have parties under the moon?
They ribbit and croak to their own tune.
Illuminate, with delicate flair,
Our world of whimsy, beyond compare!

So let's drift down these winding streams,
With lanterns aglow and playful dreams.
For fun's a boat that never sinks,
In our wild heart, it boldly links!

Roaming Through Fields of Imagination

In fields of thought, I skip and twirl,
Where candy trees sprout and whirl.
Each flower giggles with vibrant hues,
Dancing along with sparkly shoes!

A butterfly insists it can sing,
While cows debate the best ice cream thing.
I chase the clouds with a bright blue kite,
Hoping they land for a picnic delight!

Marshmallow mountains rise up tall,
With rivers of chocolate, and a cannibal ball.
A sprinkle of laughter fills the air,
As giggles flow freely everywhere!

So let us roam, unbound and free,
Through fields of fun, just you and me.
With wild thoughts that tickle the breeze,
In this land of dreams, do as you please!

Sanctuary of the Soaring Crows

In a tree of giggles, the crows hang out,
They gossip and caw, without a doubt.
With beaks of humor and feathers of cheer,
They toast to life with a friendly leer!

Raiding picnics like real pros,
Knocking off sandwiches with cheeky throws.
Their sanctuary of shenanigans shines,
With pranks that tickle and funny signs!

What secrets they share, under the sun,
As winged comedians, they crack jokes for fun.
A sanctuary of laughter, wing-flapping high,
Where even the flowers seem to sigh!

So here I'll stay, with my crow friends near,
Encircled by joy and silly cheer.
For in every flap, and every caw,
Life's a circus, with endless awe!

Unrestrained Whispers in the Wilderness

In a forest, squirrels dance with glee,
Chasing shadows of a dancing bee,
They chatter about the tree's new hat,
While I just chuckle at the silly spat.

The leaves gossip tales of hidden snacks,
While raccoons plan to raid the knickknacks,
But I just sip my juice, amused and bright,
As nature laughs at my delight in fright.

A deer in boots prances down the way,
Wearing sunglasses as it steals the day,
"Who's the fashionable?" I hear it ask,
I solemnly nod, accepting the task.

With every rustle, laughter fills the air,
Nature's circus exists without a care,
I'll stay right here, sipping to my heart's content,
Watching the wild artistry, heaven-sent.

Wild Inspirations in Silken Breezes

The butterflies wear ties, oh what a sight,
While bumblebees debate the day and night,
A grasshopper's humor hops in place,
Making giggles out of nature's embrace.

A breeze tickles flowers, making them giggle,
While ants perform a synchronized wiggle,
"Who's our judge?" the beetles call in jest,
As the wind crowns them the quirky best.

The sun plays peekaboo with a cloud,
While raindrops laugh like they're in a crowd,
"Catch us if you can!" they tease delightfully,
As puddles form a dance floor, sprightly.

In this whimsical world, joy feels so free,
As critters create their own symphony,
I'll join the fun, forming silly rhymes,
With Mother Nature, we'll laugh through the times.

Casting Dreams into the Abyss

Into the depths, I toss my old shoe,
Hoping it lands with dreams overdue,
A fish surfaces, giggling so bright,
"Not quite what I ordered, but what a sight!"

Seahorses wear crowns made of seaweed,
Debating who's the ocean's top breed,
"Did you hear the latest coral gossip?"
"Oh yes, it's a bubble, a tiny drop!"

Crabs moonwalk on the sandy shore,
Performing their antics, always wanting more,
"Move over, starfish, it's my time to gleam!"
As tides laugh at my once-serious dream.

With shells as my audience, I take my bow,
Nature applauds, though I can't hear how,
For in this abyss, laughter reigns supreme,
As I whisper my dreams to the ocean's gleam.

The Garden of Forgotten Fables

In a garden where gnomes can't sit still,
They play hide and seek with a daffodil,
"Ready or not, here we come!" they shout,
As butterflies prance, swirling about.

The daisies share tales of a knight in dread,
Whose armor rusted from the tears he shed,
"His heart was pure, but his sword was dull,
He fought off shadows, yet felt so full."

Tomatoes throw shade at the carrots nearby,
"Why so serious?" they ask with a sigh,
While peas roll their eyes, giggling with cheer,
As veggies unite for a theatrical leer.

With laughter and whimsy, the stories unfold,
In this garden of fables, so bright and bold,
For among the weeds, joy finds a way,
To share its wild fables, come out and play!

www.ingramcontent.com/pod-product-compliance
Lightning Source LLC
Chambersburg PA
CBHW070315120526
44590CB00017B/2691